KENTUCKY BOURBON BARONS

LEGENDARY DISTILLERS FROM THE GOLDEN AGE OF WHISKEY MAKING

ISBN 978-1-935497-92-9

Printed in the United States of America
Book design by Carly Schnur

Published by Butler Books
P.O. Box 7311
Louisville, Kentucky 40257
phone: (502) 897-9393
fax: (502) 897-9797
www.butlerbooks.com

KENTUCKY BOURBON BARONS

LEGENDARY DISTILLERS FROM THE GOLDEN AGE OF WHISKEY MAKING

CHESTER ZOELLER

KENTUCKY BOURBON BARONS

KENTUCKY BOURBON BARONS

Kentucky has long been blessed with individuals and families renowned for their ability to produce superior bourbon. While doing research for my book *Bourbon in Kentucky, A History of Distilleries in Kentucky,* I found that a number of these people were involved in more than one distillery during their lifetimes. They were the true "Bourbon Barons," Kentuckians who shaped the industry throughout its growth and development. During the past 225 years or so, there have been about 2,500 registered distilleries in Kentucky. What will remain unknown is how many moonshine operations there have been during that time.

This book is an effort to bring to your attention as many of the Bourbon Barons and their distilleries as possible. I have included the distilleries with which they were involved, the years of the Barons' involvement, the distilleries' locations, and, when known, their years of operation. (For a more complete description of each distillery, I refer you to my book *Bourbon in Kentucky.*)

A BIT OF BACKGROUND

The vast majority of these Barons were distilling bourbon in the period between the Civil War and Prohibition. Before the Civil War, most whiskey was produced by farmer-distillers or millers. After Prohibition, the distilleries were usually owned by large corporations—no longer by families. This was the time that many think of as the golden age of distilling. The distilleries were producing both sweet mash and sour mash bourbon, as well as rye and whiskies made from a variety of grains.

There were about 300 large distilleries during this span, but the actual number of owners was considerably smaller. The average adult, male and female, consumed 2.4 gallons of spirits each year. That does not include the more than 11 gallons of beer that on average each American drank during this period.

Before Prohibition, some distilleries devoted their entire production to the sweet mash method, in which distillers used fresh yeast in each batch. This method produced a sweeter flavor than that of sour mash. At Prohibition, almost all sweet mash production stopped.

All present-day distillers use the sour mash method of distilling. This method uses a small amount of previously fermented mash (said to be sour) that is added to the next batch. It may be called "backset" or "setback," and, as in the case of preparing sourdough bread, it helps maintain the quality of the yeast from batch to batch. It is not required or even necessary in the production of bourbon. Whether or not a brand states on its label that it is a sour mash whiskey, today all brands are sour mash.

Beginning in about 1862, every distillery in the United States was given a Registered Distillery (RD) number. Each state was divided into districts, and each distillery within each district was given a specific number in order for the government to monitor its whiskey production and collect taxes accordingly. The government subsequently replaced RD numbers with Distilled Spirits Plant (DSP) numbers. Therefore, each distillery mentioned in this book was assigned either an RD or a DSP number.

It is important to keep in mind that distilling experienced boom and bust periods throughout its history. Much of its problem was caused by overproduction in the boom years. Its effects were compounded by the very deep recession of 1893, Prohibition, and World War II— when distilleries were forced to stop making whiskey and instead make industrial alcohol for the war effort. It is little wonder that so many distilleries were bought and sold on a regular basis.

After Prohibition, the bourbon business failed to recover its former glory. Between 1980 and 2000, the industry was in great decline. Since then, it has made a remarkable comeback. It may interest readers to know there are more barrels of whiskey—about 4.8 million—than there are people in Kentucky—about 4.6 million.

Many other outstanding distillery proprietors were involved with perhaps one or two distilleries, but they are not among the Barons in this book.

There were a few exceptions to the general time period between the Civil War and Prohibition, and my first family of Barons is one of them.

SNYDER FAMILY
BOONE, TRIMBLE, AND CARROLL COUNTIES

Two of the very early Bourbon Barons to distill whiskey in Kentucky were the Snyder brothers, William and John, of Boone County and, later, of both Trimble and Carroll counties.

Upon the death of Michael Snyder of Virginia, his estate listed six copper stills and all the other equipment needed to run a large distilling operation. (George Washington, reputed to be the largest distiller of his day, also used six stills at Mount Vernon.) Two of Michael's sons, William and John, made their way to Petersburg, in Boone County on the Ohio River. There they bought a large steam mill and, in 1836, started distilling whiskey. Their distillery initially was operated as the Petersburg Distillery and later as the Boone County Distillery, which they developed into the largest distillery in Kentucky at the time. By 1860, it had produced 1.125 million gallons of whiskey—about 22,500 barrels annually, or 150 barrels per day. Actually, because it was too hot to distill in the summers in those days (the yeast would die before it could start the fermentation process), the number of barrels produced per day was even greater. The distillery had its own cooperage and employed 16 coopers to keep up with production. After experiencing financial difficulties, William sold the distillery in 1862 to his son-in-law, William Appleton, and others. Ultimately, the plant was sold to the Whiskey Trust in 1888, and it was closed by 1900.

In 1843, the brothers built a distillery near Milton in Trimble County, and in the following year, John was killed in an accident at the distillery. Thereafter, William was joined by his son, William T. Snyder, and they grew the plant into a large concern that was known as the

Petersburg Distillery

William Snyder
Courtesy of Boone County Library

Richwood Distillery. The plant was later known as Snyder Brothers, Tea Kettle, Susquemac, and Susquehanne. The distillery could mash some 1,300 bushels per day, and its warehouse capacity was 68,000 barrels. The distillery was operated for many years by James O. Snyder, John's son, and it closed at Prohibition.

In 1849, James S. Snyder, son of William, and William's son-in-law, William Appleton, built a distillery in Carrollton, Carroll County, on the banks of the Ohio River. The distillery was destroyed by fire in 1854 and lost some 5,200 barrels of whiskey. The plant was rebuilt and in operation until 1859.

After leaving Petersburg, just before the start of the Civil War, William and his family moved to Chattanooga, Tennessee, where he purchased another distillery that he ran until it was destroyed by the Union Army.

Eagle Distillery

MONARCH FAMILY
DAVIESS COUNTY

Daviess County is a prime example of family dynasties in the distilling business. In fact, the county was blessed with two such families, one in the latter half of the nineteenth century and a second in the first half of the twentieth century.

When most of us think of the heritage of distilling, we think of the Irish or the Scots. However, when reviewing the history of Daviess County, we find that the French gave us the Monarch family. After leaving France, the family settled in Maryland, where the patriarch, Francis Monarch, died. Thomas, the seventh child, was born one month after his father's death and, three weeks later, was on his way to Kentucky. The family stopped in Louisville before making its way to Washington County, where Thomas was raised and married. In 1834, he moved to Daviess County, where and he and his wife had 10 children. Of the eight who were boys, one died as a child, one died while a very young man, and the remaining six went on to own one or more distilleries in Daviess County. The Monarch brothers simply followed the family's tradition of distilling, which it had done for generations in France.

The first of Thomas Monarch's sons to open a distillery in Daviess County was Thomas J., at age 23. In 1859, he built a distillery on the Green River at Birk City that originally was known as the T. J. Monarch Distillery, Registered Distillery (RD) #16. Its mashing capacity was 100 bushels per day. Thereafter, it was known as the Cliff Falls Distillery and then the Eagle Distillery. After it was sold to J. W. McCullough, it became the very famous Green River Distillery.

In about 1861, Thomas J. Monarch purchased a distillery that had been built by W. L. Berry. In 1868, he moved it to Grissom's Landing on

M. V. Monarch

M. V. Monarch Distillery

the Ohio River. It was also first known as the T. J. Monarch Distillery, RD #8, although the name was soon changed to the Eagle Distillery. The distillery could mash 500 bushels per day. Thomas died in 1887 at age 51.

M. V. Monarch was a very active distillery owner and operator. In 1867, he built the M. V. Monarch Distillery, RD #17, which thereafter was known as the Sour Mash Distillery. The distillery could mash some 200 bushels per day. In 1870, M. V. hired a salesman named Peter (P. E.) Payne. He was to become not only his vice president, but his brother-in-law as well. M. V. later purchased the John Hanning Distillery, RD #11, which had been consolidated with the E. C. Berry Distillery, RD #33. This plant could mash 1,200 bushels per day, and its warehouse capacity was 50,000 barrels. M. V. Monarch also had an interest in the Cliff Falls Distillery, RD #16. In 1877, he was associated with his brother Richard and E. P. Millett in a wholesale liquor business known as Monarch Brothers and Millett.

M. V. was a director of the First National Bank of Owensboro, director of a gravel company, and an Owensboro city councilman.

Richard Monarch was perhaps the most active of the Monarch brothers in the distillery business. In 1869, he and his brother Daniel built and operated the D. Monarch Distillery, RD #24. The distillery was capable of mashing 400 bushels per day. After Daniel died in 1875, Richard continued its operation until 1890. The plant was then sold to James Thompson of Louisville, a cousin of George Garvin Brown of Brown-Forman fame. The distillery was also known as H. S. Barton, and it would become best known as Glenmore.

In 1881, Richard Monarch purchased the Eagle Distillery, RD #8, after the death of his brother Thomas. In 1885, Richard purchased the Daviess County Distillery, RD #2, which could mash 800 bushels per day and could store 32,000 barrels of whiskey. In 1901, he sold the distillery to George Medley of Bardstown, Dick Meschendorf of Louisville, and Henry Edelen. In the late 1890s, Richard Monarch purchased the E. W. Murphy Distillery, RD #20. This was a small distillery that could mash only 60 bushels per day and store 1,500 barrels. It has been suggested

Daviess County Distillery
Courtesy of Oscar Getz Museum

Glenmore Distillery
Courtesy of Kentucky Historical Society

Daviess County Distillery
Courtesy of Oscar Getz Museum

that he bought this operation so that he and his friends would have an adequate supply of their favorite elixir.

William H. Monarch, Richard Monarch, and E. P. Millett were the owners of the E. P. Millett Distillery, RD #13. The distillery was located in Owensboro and could mash 350 bushels per day.

Sylvester I. Monarch built a distillery about 1870 that was first known as the S. I. Monarch Distillery, RD #10. This small plant could mash only 100 bushels per day and store 1,500 barrels. The distillery would become the Hill and Hill Distillery and, still later, the Rock Spring Distillery. In 1880, Sylvester I. Monarch was an owner with his brother, Thomas J., in the Eagle Distillery, RD #8, and the Cliff Falls Distillery, RD #16. Sylvester married another sister of M.V.'s wife, thereby becoming brother-in-law to not only M. V., but to P. E. Payne as well.

The Monarch brothers, owners of some of the largest, best known distilleries in the state in the late 1800s, were a true dynasty.

John A. Medley, Edwin Wathen Medley, George E. Medley II

R. Wathen Medley, Thomas A. Medley Jr., Ben F. Medley II

MEDLEY FAMILY
DAVIESS COUNTY

The second Daviess County family to have a great impact on the distilling business was the Medley family. When the first Medley, John, came to America in 1634, he brought his still with him. By 1800, John IV had settled in Washington County, Kentucky, and he too had carried his still to his new home. George Medley was born in 1850, and in 1898, he became involved in the Mattingly & Moore Distillery, RD #272, in Bardstown.

By 1901, George had purchased the Daviess County Distillery with Dick Meschendorf of Louisville, owner of the Old Kentucky Distillery, RD #354. At this time, the plant could mash 500 bushels per day, and its warehouse could store 32,000 barrels. After the death of Meschendorf, George became sole owner of the distillery. His son, Thomas A., became president of the company after George's death in 1910. The distillery survived Prohibition by becoming a concentration house—one of 10 such locations in Kentucky where all of the whiskey in the state was stored during Prohibition. In 1928, the distillery, whiskey, and brands were sold to the American Medicinal Spirits Company, which was controlled by the Wathen family, which will be discussed later.

Thomas A. Medley joined his family with the Wathen family when he married the daughter of Richard N. Wathen in 1902. Thomas and Florence had six sons, all of whom were involved in the distilling business. They were R. Wathen, George E., Thomas A. Jr., John A., Ben F., and Edward Wathen Medley.

In 1933, the Medleys' Daviess County Distilling Company purchased the Old Rock Springs Distilling Company, Distilled Spirits Plant (DSP) #10, which was next to their original distillery. The plant was capable of mashing 3,000 bushels per day, and its warehouse could store 200,000 barrels. In 1940, the distillery was sold to Fleischmann and during that year, Thomas died. The remaining Medley brothers immediately bought the old Green River Distillery, DSP #49, which was very close to the Old Rock Springs Distillery, and began distilling once again. The plant could mash 2,000 bushels per day and had warehouse capacity for 180,000 barrels. In 1959, the distillery was sold to Renfield Importers of New York, although John and Wathen Medley continued operating it. The following year, Ben and Tom Medley built a distillery at Stanley named the Old Stanley Distillery. The distillery operated for only a year.

In 1976, the Medley Distilling Company bought the Old Hoffman Distillery, DSP #112, in Anderson County, and the Ezra Brooks brand. In 1979, Medley bought the 21 Brands Distillery, DSP #32, near Frankfort. In 1988, the Medley Distilling Company was acquired by Glenmore, thereby bringing to an end another bourbon dynasty.

THIXTON AND MILLETT COMPANY
DAVIESS COUNTY

While not a family firm, the ownership of Thixton and Millett certainly qualifies as a Baron. Its owners were E. P. Millett of Owensboro and John Thixton of Louisville.

Millett got his start in the wholesale whiskey business in 1877 as a member of the firm of Monarch Brothers and Millett in Owensboro. The firm consisted of E. P. Millett, and M. V. and Richard Monarch. Millett married into the Monarch family when he wed Etta Monarch, the daughter of Thomas J. In 1881, he was the owner and operator of the E. P. Millett Distillery, RD #13, in Owensboro, with his brother, Melvin F. Millett. The distillery could mash some 350 bushels per day. The distillery was later sold to Richard Monarch.

By the early 1880s, E. P. Millett and Company was the owner of the Glenmore Distillery, RD #24, also in Owensboro. E. P. Millett, Richard Monarch and William H. Monarch headed the firm.

In the 1890s, Millett had an interest in the Old Best Distillery, RD #99, located in Hancock County. This was a small plant with the capacity to mash 100 barrels daily. By 1900, he had moved to Henderson, where he purchased an interest in the Worsham Distillery, RD #50. He subsequently sold his interest in the distillery to Henry Kraver and returned to Owensboro. Shortly thereafter, he purchased the Spring Water Distillery, RD #4, in Bowling Green. This plant could mash 500 bushels per day. In 1902, E. P. Millett had become established in Louisville in the wholesale liquor business.

John Thixton, a native of Louisville, moved to Owensboro with his family when he was 15 years old. By 1882, he was a member of the firm of Thixton and Slaughter, a wholesale liquor company in Louisville.

That year the firm established the John Thixton Distillery, RD #30, one mile east of the Daviess County Courthouse in Owensboro. The plant could mash about 300 bushels per day and could store about 2,500 barrels. The plant burned in 1886 and was not rebuilt. The partners also owned a two-fifths interest in the E. C. Berry Distillery, RD #33, also in Owensboro. Their partners were A. F. Berryman, W. H. Perkins, and Alex Hill, the latter two being Hill and Perkins, the successors to E. C. Berry. The E.C. Berry plant burned in 1887.

In 1888, Thixton also had an interest in a distillery, RD #30, near Leach in Grayson County.

Although he was from Louisville, John Thixton became mayor of Owensboro in 1878. He also served on either the school board or city council for 10 years. He was president of the Bank of Commerce, a director of the U. S. National Bank, and organizer of the Central City Bank.

John Thixton joined with E. P. Millett in 1889 to form the Thixton, Millett and Company, a wholesale liquor firm in Louisville. From 1887 to 1893, they owned the Glenmore Distillery, RD #24, in Owensboro.

By 1903, they had purchased the Boone Brothers Distillery, RD #422, near Bardstown. This was a very small operation that mashed only about 70 bushels per day and had warehouse capacity for some 2,600 barrels. In 1912, the firm purchased the Old Saxton (Blair) Distillery, RD #375, in Chicago (now St. Francis), in Marion County. This small plant could mash about 100 bushels per day. This distillery operated until Prohibition.

After his death in 1894, his wife had a life-size statue carved from Italian marble placed at his grave site. It still stands in the Elmwood Cemetery in Owensboro.

PEPPER FAMILY
WOODFORD AND FAYETTE COUNTIES

Around 1780, Elijah Pepper came to Kentucky with his brother-in-law, John O'Bannon. He may have started distilling at the site of what would become the Old Pepper Spring near Lexington on the Frankfort Pike. By 1797, Elijah and John were operating a distillery in Versailles, just below a large spring behind the Woodford County courthouse. In about 1812, the partnership dissolved and Elijah built a new distillery near Millville, on Glenns Creek, about 10 miles southeast of Frankfort. The distillery could mash about 125 bushels per day, and its warehouse could store 9,000 barrels.

In 1825, Elijah's son Oscar took over operation of the plant. Elijah died in 1831, and soon thereafter Oscar had the good fortune to employ James Crow as his distiller. Crow, a Scot, was a man of some learning, and by use of his scientific methods he perfected the sour mash method of distilling. Their whiskey subsequently became famous throughout the United States. Two of their best customers were Henry Clay and Daniel Webster.

Oscar Pepper built a second distillery that he named the Old Crow Distillery, RD #106, in honor of James Crow. Initially, the plant could mash 500 bushels per day and store 25,000 barrels. The distillery was just downstream on Glenns Creek, near its mouth at the Kentucky River. The Old Crow Distillery was purchased by W. A. Gains and Company, of which Taylor was a member, about 1873.

Upon Oscar's death in 1865, E. H. Taylor became executor of his estate and guardian of Oscar's minor son, James E. Pepper. James, with the guidance of E. H. Taylor, began operating the distillery about 1872. Taylor sold the distillery to George T. Stagg in 1878. Stagg sold the distillery to Leopold Labrot and James H. Graham in about 1880, and they operated it until shortly before Prohibition. After Prohibition the distillery was reopened as Labrot & Graham and was owned by R. A. Baker. In 1940, Brown-Forman purchased the plant and closed it soon thereafter. Years later and after spending millions of dollars on its refurbishment, which included three pot stills, in 1996 they reopened the distillery as Labrot & Graham. In 2004, its name was changed to Woodford Reserve Distillery, DSP #2. It is situated in a small glen in the Bluegrass horse country, a picturesque site, and it is well worth a visit.

In 1879, James E. Pepper purchased the Headley and Farra Distillery, RD #5, in Lexington. This may have been the site of the very first Pepper distillery in Kentucky. Its motto, "Born with the Republic," indicated that its establishment coincided with the nation's independence. The James E. Pepper distillery grew into a very large concern, and its products were known across the United States. Before Prohibition, the plant could mash 1,000 bushels a day, and its warehouse capacity was 50,000 barrels. It became a concentration warehouse during-Prohibition, and, near its end, the plant was allowed to make whiskey to replenish that which was sold for medicinal purposes.

In 1885, James E. Pepper purchased the Silver Springs Distillery, RD #46, near Yarnallton in Fayette County. This plant was also known as the Little Pepper Distillery. It had mashing capacity of 200 bushels and storage for 10,000 barrels of whiskey.

Robert P. Pepper, a cousin of Oscar and nephew of Elijah, operated a distillery on the Kentucky River at Frankfort. It was known as the R. P. Pepper Distillery, RD #1. It was in operation from about 1862 to 1878, when it was purchased by the Newcomb-Buchanan Company, RD #368, in Louisville.

James E. Pepper

Oscar Pepper Distillery
Courtesy of Kentucky Historical Society

Old Crow Distillery

E. H. Taylor Jr.

O. F. C. Distillery
Courtesy of Kentucky Historical Society

E. H. TAYLOR JR.
FRANKLIN COUNTY

The man whom many consider the most outstanding in the distilling business was Edmund H. Taylor Jr. He was a native Kentuckian, a grandnephew of General Zachary Taylor, and a descendant of James Madison. His distilleries were a pleasure to behold, and he insisted on a quality product.

Taylor was a staunch supporter of the Bottled-in-Bond Act, which was passed in 1897. This law almost guaranteed that the whiskey that left the distillery was the same whiskey that reached the consumer. The act required that whiskey be placed in a federally supervised warehouse, that the whiskey age for a minimum of four years, that the product be at least 100 proof, and that the distiller's name appear on the bottle.

Taylor, a banker, entered the whiskey business in 1860 as a member of Gains, Berry and Company. The firm's other members were William Gains and Hiram Berry. After the Civil War, the firm was reorganized as W. A. Gains and Company, and it had the same principles as before.

In 1869, Taylor purchased a distillery in Leestown, on the Kentucky River, and renamed it the O. F. C. (Old Fire Copper) Distillery, RD #2. When rebuilt, the distillery was a state-of-the-art facility that could mash 500 bushels per day and store some 45,000 barrels of whiskey. Soon thereafter, Taylor built a second distillery next to O. F. C., which he named the Carlisle Distillery, RD #113. It was of equal size, could mash 500 bushels a day, and had warehouse storage for 35,000 barrels. The site became a concentration warehouse during Prohibition and near its end was allowed to make whiskey. These distilleries are still in operation and are known today as Buffalo Trace.

In 1870, W. A. Gains and Company built the Hermitage Distillery, RD #4, in south Frankfort, on the banks of the Kentucky River. The distillery could mash 1,000 bushels a day and had warehouse storage for 48,000 barrels.

In 1873, W. A. Gains and Company purchased the previously mentioned Old Crow Distillery, RD #106, in Woodford County on Glenns Creek.

In 1879, Edmund Taylor's son, Jacob Swigert Taylor, bought a small distillery located next to the Old Crow Distillery. In 1882, he sold the distillery to his father, who renamed it the Old Taylor Distillery, RD #53. It was in a picturesque valley on Glenns Creek. The distillery could mash 175 bushels per day and could store 8,200 barrels. Taylor knew how to promote his product; he built a stone castle for his offices and a beautiful enclosure for his spring. His company built a railroad from Frankfort to the distillery, which allowed him to bring large numbers of people to the Old Taylor Distillery.

In 1885, Edmund Taylor purchased the Old McBrayer Distillery, RD #17, near Mt. Sterling in Montgomery County. The plant could mash 200 bushels a day and had storage for 16,000 barrels.

All three of his sons—Swigert, Edmond, and Kenner—were involved in the whiskey business. In 1933, Kenner bought the Frankfort Distillery, RD #33, at the Forks of Elk Creek. Now known as the Old Grand-Dad Distillery, it is owned by Jim Beam.

Taylor served 16 years as mayor of Frankfort. He served two terms in the Kentucky House of Representatives and one in the Senate. He became an outstanding breeder of both Hereford cattle and Thoroughbred horses. The father of eight children, Taylor lived to age 93. He was also quite a dandy—as can be seen in the photo above.

Hermitage Distillery
Courtesy of Kentucky Historical Society

Old Grand-Dad Distillery

J. Swigert Taylor

Old Taylor Distillery

WATHEN FAMILY
MARION, BULLITT, AND JEFFERSON COUNTIES

One of the most influential families ever involved in the whiskey business was the Wathen family. Henry Hudson Wathen came to Kentucky from Maryland before 1788. He settled in Marion County and started distilling on the Rolling Fork River, near Lebanon. His youngest son, Richard, became involved in the business and, about 1852, built a small distillery at Calvary. In about 1875, two of Richard's sons, John Bernard (J. B.) and R. N. (Nick), built a distillery at Lebanon, which became known as the Rolling Fork Distillery, RD #270. This distillery, which could mash about 100 bushels per day, produced a sweet mash whiskey.

In 1879, the Wathens took in two partners, H. Mueller and Charles Kobert, and built a second distillery on the site that was known as the Cumberland Distillery, RD #299. This distillery produced only sour mash whiskey.

In 1880, J. B. and his brothers, R. N. (Nick) and M. A. (Nace), built a large distillery in Louisville known as the J. B. Wathen and Bro. Distillery, RD #363. The distillery could mash 175 bushels per day and could store about 50,000 barrels.

In 1899, the three brothers purchased the Hayden Distillery, RD #420, at Hobbs in Bullitt County, and renamed it the Old Grand-Dad Distillery, which produced a very popular brand. The distillery could mash 400 bushels a day.

In 1900, J. B.'s sons—R. E., O. H., and J. B Jr.— built a large distillery in Shively, just south of Louisville. It was known as the R. E. Wathen Distillery, RD #19. Its mashing capacity was about 2,500 bushels per day, and its warehouse could store 75,000 barrels.

Rolling Fork Distillery
Courtesy of University of Louisville

Old Grand-Dad Distillery
Courtesy of Norvelle Wathen

R. E. Wathen Distillery

When Prohibition came into effect, the Wathens had a great deal of whiskey on hand in their warehouses. Sensing an opportunity, they purchased many of the great brands, as well as additional stocks of whiskey. Many warehouses across Kentucky were full of whiskey that the owners were willing to sell to the Wathens, who subsequently established the American Medicinal Spirits Company (AMS). The firm was allowed to bottle and sell whiskey for medicinal purposes during Prohibition, when it was the largest supplier of whiskey. AMS later evolved into National Distillers.

After Prohibition was repealed, John A. Wathen, a cousin, rebuilt the Cumberland Distillery, RD #299, in Lebanon. The plant could mash 800 bushels a day, and it had warehouse storage for 95,000 barrels.

T. J. Megibben

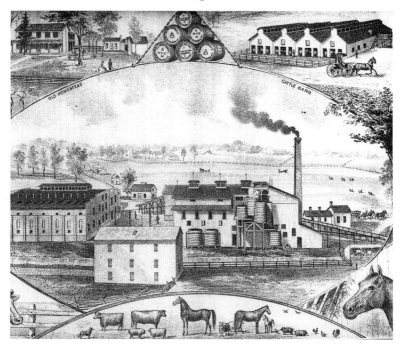

Edgewater Distillery

T. J. MEGIBBEN AND FAMILY
HARRISON COUNTY

One word can describe T. J. Megibben: capitalist. Another three words complete the description: self-made man. Starting with nothing, Megibben became a farmer and eventually owned more than 2,800 acres in Harrison County. He became an outstanding breeder of short-horned cattle, which could cost as much as $25,000 each. He had more than 50 head of Thoroughbred race horses and 100 trotting horses. He was one of the first in the country to build a stock of the leading breeds of sheep.

T. J. Megibben served in the Kentucky House of Representatives for eight years and thereafter in the State Senate for two terms. He served as president of the Kentucky Union Railroad, the Kentucky Horse Breeders Association and the Short-Horn Cattle Breeders Association, and as president of Latonia Racetrack from 1881 until his death. He was also owner of Springbok, winner of the 1873 Belmont Race.

Harrison County was known for its many fine distilleries. Many of them were owned at one time or another by T. J. Megibben. He started as a common hand in the distilling business, then became an assistant distiller and, finally, head distiller. In 1855, as a member of Shawhan, Snell and Megibben, he leased a distillery that was four and one-half miles southwest of Cynthiana. Three years later, he bought the distillery, which was known as the Edgewater Distillery, RD #1. In the early 1880s, he was joined by his brother, James K. Megibben, and they operated the distillery until T. J.'s death in 1900. The distillery could mash 400 bushels a day and had storage for 25,000 barrels.

In 1868, T. J. and James K. Megibben purchased the Excelsior Distillery, RD #38. It was three and one-half miles south of Cynthiana on the South Branch of the Licking River. The distillery could mash 700

Old Lewis Hunter Distillery

Felix S. Ashbrook

bushels per day and could store 17,500 barrels.

T. J. Megibben and William Tarr purchased the Ashland Distillery, RD #1, on Frankfort Pike and Town Branch, near Lexington in 1868. In 1879, the firm was reorganized with Sam Clay Jr. and Joseph M. Kimbrough, T. J.'s son-in-law, taking minority interests.

In 1880, T. J. and James K. Megibben bought the Old Lewis Hunter Distillery, RD #19, next to the Excelsior Distillery. The distillery could mash 140 bushels per day and had storage for 15,000 barrels. Soon after E. W. Bramble married T. J.'s daughter Loraine, he became a partner in the firm of Megibben, Bramble and Company, which operated the distillery. When T. J. died, his brother James K. continued to operate it until it was sold to the Whiskey Trust in 1902.

In 1880, T. J.—who with Felix S. Ashbrook and E. W. Bramble was part of the firm of F. S. Ashbrook—bought the Van Hook Distillery, RD #35, one mile north of the Harrison County Courthouse. The plant could mash 200 bushels per day and had storage for 11,000 barrels. He sold it to Felix S. Ashbrook in 1888.

In 1884, T. J. Megibben purchased the Paris Distillery, RD #77, one mile northeast of the Bourbon County Courthouse. The distillery mashed 500 bushels per day and could store 20,000 barrels of whiskey. Megibben operated the plant until his death in 1900, by which time he had been involved in at least six large distilleries. He is credited with creating the Old Fashioned cocktail at the Pendennis Club in Louisville.

B. F. Mattingly Distillery
Courtesy of the Oscar Getz Museum

MATTINGLY BROTHERS
AND DAVID L. GRAVES
MARION COUNTY

Brothers John G. and Benjamin F. Mattingly of Marion County started distilling in Marion County in 1845. Their distillery may have been the first registered distillery in Kentucky. In 1860, the brothers built a distillery on the banks of the Muddy Fork of Beargrass Creek near Hamilton Street (now Lexington Road), in Jefferson County. In 1867, the brothers sold this plant to David L. Graves, also of Marion County. They then moved their distillery to the Oakland area of Louisville, about where Seventh and Hill Street are today. In 1874, they again moved the distillery when they built a large plant at Rudd Avenue and High Street (now Northwestern Parkway) in the west end of Louisville. It was known as the John G. Mattingly and Brothers Distillery, RD #2. This distillery could mash 2,000 bushels per day and had warehouse capacity for 56,000 barrels. A second distillery at this location, known as the Chamberlain Distillery, was destroyed by flood in 1884. John was the senior member of the firm of John G. Mattingly and Brothers Distillery and Ben, the junior member.

In 1878, Ben sold his interest in the concern and established his own distillery, the Marion County Distillery, RD #372. The distillery was on 32nd Street, between Missouri Avenue and Rudd Avenue, in the Portland area of Louisville. It had the capacity to produce 30,000 barrels a year.

John was joined by his sons, Columbus G. and Ben G., and the name of the firm was changed to John G. Mattingly and Sons Distillery. John is given credit for perfecting the columnar coffee still that allowed for continuous distilling, unlike the pot still that could only distill small amounts of mash at a time. In 1890, the firm was reorganized, and Paul

Jones was made president. Jones would later become president of the Frankfort Distillery and owner of the famous Four Roses brand.

John Mattingly also owned the Glendale Distillery, RD #6, at 34th Street and Tyler Avenue in Louisville's west end. The latter plant was built about 1883. The plant could mash 200 bushels a day and had capacity to store 27,500 barrels. The distillery later became the Bonnie Brothers Distillery and later still, Park and Tilford.

Ben was also the owner of the B. F. Mattingly Distillery, RD #14, near St. Mary in Marion County. The distillery could mash about 200 bushels per day. For about 30 years, J. T. S. Brown and Brother bought the distillery's production. In 1902, the Brown-Forman Company was formed, and it bought a minority interest in the distillery. The distillery had almost no warehousing, and the product was shipped to Louisville and stored at the White Mills Distillery, which Brown-Forman had purchased.

Ben Mattingly was a partner with Tom Moore and Richard Cummins in the Mattingly & Moore Distillery, RD #272, in Bardstown. The plant could mash 250 bushels per day and had warehouse storage for 7,500 barrels. In 1889, Tom Moore left and started his own distillery next to this plant.

In his later years, Ben Mattingly was deeply in debt and unable to pay his creditors. His brother John, on the other hand, seemed to be financially secure, and he died with a substantial estate.

David L. Graves sold the distillery on Beargrass Creek in Louisville to Beall, Stiles and Company, also of Marion County, in 1868. He soon thereafter bought a distillery on Lexington Road at Grinstead Drive and renamed it the Mayflower Distillery, RD #354. Graves had owned distilleries at both Raywick and Lebanon in Marion County. He had produced the brands Ashton and Mayflower at those locations and brought them with him to the Louisville distillery. The Mayflower Distillery's name was changed to Old Kentucky Distillery when Dick Meschendorf purchased it in 1892.

Old Kentucky Distillery

In 1867, David L. Graves built a distillery in Uniontown in Union County. At the time of his ownership it could mash 400 bushels per day, and its warehouse could store 10,000 barrels. He named it the Union County Distillery, RD #6, and shortly thereafter sold it to J. M. Lancaster. He, in turn, sold it to John G. Roach of Louisville.

DIETRICH (DICK) MESCHENDORF
JEFFERSON COUNTY

In 1889, Dick Meschendorf, Charles Lemmon, and A. W. Bierbaum became owners of the Old Times Distillery, RD #297, on the northeast corner of 28th and Broadway in Louisville. The plant could mash 150 bushels per day and had warehouse storage for 25,000 barrels. The distillery would later be known as the Number One Distillery. In 1897, Meschendorf sold his interest in the plant and purchased the Mayflower Distillery, RD #354, which was at the intersection of Lexington Road and Grinstead Drive in Louisville. At that time, the distillery was mashing 1,500 bushels per day and had warehouse capacity for 65,000 barrels. As noted above, Meschendorf changed its name to the Old Kentucky Distillery. It was moved to Shively after Prohibition and then sold to the Brown-Forman Company in 1940. Brown-Forman renamed it the Early Times Distillery.

Meschendorf was an owner and vice-president of the Pleasure Ridge Park Distillery, RD #413, on Dixie Highway in Pleasure Ridge Park. It had three warehouses with capacity for 30,000 barrels. In 1896, the distillery was sold to the Bernheim Brothers.

In the 1890s, Meschendorf was involved with the Eminence Distillery, RD #107, in Eminence, Henry County. The distillery could mash 300 bushels per day and could store 10,000 barrels.

In 1901, George E. Medley of Bardstown, Henry Edelen, and Dick Meschendorf purchased the Daviess County Distillery, RD #10, from Richard Monarch. The distillery was in Owensboro, on the banks of the Ohio River. In 1903, Medley bought out his two partners.

Meschendorf earned a fine reputation in the whiskey business. In the early 1900s, he was twice called to Washington, DC, in connection with the attempt to pass the Pure Food and Drug Act (1906). The act was aimed in part at stopping the adulteration of distillers' products by the unscrupulous rectifiers and saloon keepers of the time. He met with both President Theodore Roosevelt and President William H. Taft to discuss the merits of the Act.

Meschendorf died in 1911 at the age of 53.

JOHN G. ROACH
JEFFERSON COUNTY

John G. Roach entered the distilling business in 1864 as part of the firm that owned the Rugby Distillery, RD #360, in Louisville. The firm consisted of Roach, H. A. Thierman, and perhaps Ben Mattingly. Roach operated the distillery under the name The American Distilling Company.

In 1878, he purchased the Lancaster and Spalding Distillery, RD #6, in Uniontown, Union County, on the banks of the Ohio River. The firm's owners were Roach, Charles P. Graves, and John Barbee. Roach changed the name to the Rich Grain Distillery. The plant was sold to the first Whiskey Trust in 1892.

Several Whiskey Trusts were created during the late 1800s and early 1900s. The first was known as the Distillers and Cattle Feeders Trust. It was created in the same way that John D. Rockefeller Sr. created the Standard Oil Company. The idea was to control the industry by buying up a substantial number of distilleries and controlling the quantity and price of the whiskey reaching the market. This trust failed for a number of reasons. A second trust was created that was known as the Kentucky Distillers and Warehouse Company. It bought up over 50 distilleries in the state, closed many of the smaller plants, and enlarged the larger ones in order to drive down the cost of production. Many fine distilleries were lost forever during this period, and once again the trust failed.

In 1881, Roach built the Old Time Distillery, RD #297, on the southeast corner of 28th and Broadway in Louisville. He and Charles P. Graves were the distillery's owners. In 1886, they sold the distillery to Andrew Biggs. This plant would become world famous as the Sunny Brook Distillery.

After selling the Rich Grain Distillery, Roach built the Old Log Cabin Distillery, RD #8, in 1893. This was a difficult time to open a

Lancaster and Spalding Distillery in Union County, Kentucky

new distillery due to a deep recession known as the Panic of 1893, and many distilleries were closed during that period. The plant was located in west Louisville at 30th Street and Garland Avenue. The distillery originally mashed 200 bushels per day and could store 32,000 barrels of whiskey. The Old Log Cabin brand became one of the most popular in the industry. Roach sold the distillery to the second Whiskey Trust in 1899 and retired.

In 1885, John G. Roach also had an ownership interest in the J. B. Wathen Distillery, RD #363, in Louisville.

There are indications that he was involved in the Sour Mash Distillery, RD #17, in Owensboro.

A. Ph. Stitzel Distillery

Courtesy of the University of Louisville

Stizel-Weller Distillery

STITZEL FAMILY
JEFFERSON COUNTY

In 1872, Jacob and Frederick Stitzel built a distillery in Louisville on 26th Street, between Broadway and Maple Street. It was named Stitzel Brothers Distillery, RD #106. The plant mashed 160 bushels per day. Their Mondamis Sour Mash brand won the Medal of Honor at the Paris Exhibition in France in 1889. Other brands were Fred Stitzel and Glencoe. In the late 1880s, they sold the plant to Phillip Hollenbach, and its name was changed to Glencoe Distillery. The Stitzel brothers continued to operate it. After Jacob's death in 1913, one of his sons, Frank H. Stitzel, operated the plant.

Frederick Stitzel patented the barrel rack system, first used in 1879, that allowed air to circulate around the barrels.

In 1880, Frederick and his brother-in-law, Jacob Laval Jr., purchased the Glen Spring Distillery Company, RD #57, on Glenns Creek in Woodford County. The distillery could mash 180 bushels per day, and its warehouse capacity was 6,000 barrels.

Jacob Stitzel's sons, Phil and Fred, left their father's distillery in 1903 and built their own plant on Story Avenue in Louisville. The A. Ph. Stitzel Distillery, RD #17, could mash 400 bushels per day and could store 25,000 barrels.

After Prohibition, Phillip J. Hollenbach's son, Louis J., reopened the Glencoe Distillery at Cane Run Road and Camp Ground Road in Shively, south of Louisville. The plant was sold to National Distilleries in 1941 and then to United Distillers, which closed the facility in 1975.

In the 1950s, the Phil Hollenbach Company bought the Bardstown Distillery, RD #47, and renamed it the Glencoe Distillery. It was later sold to Haas Brothers.

William L. Weller

William Larue Weller entered the wholesale liquor business in Louisville in 1849. He purchased whiskey from a number of distilleries and bottled under his name. In 1908, two of the firm's salesmen, Julian P. Van Winkle and Alex T. Farnsley, purchased the William L. Weller Company.

During Prohibition, the A. Ph. Stitzel Distillery became a concentration warehouse that bottled medicinal whiskey for itself and many other bulk holders. Weller obtained the Old Fitzgerald brand from S. C. Herbst, owner of the Old Judge Distillery, RD #11, during this time. In 1929, Stitzel obtained a permit to produce medicinal whiskey to replace depleted stocks, which it did from 1930 to 1933.

At Prohibition's end, the A. Ph. Stitzel Distillery and the William L. Weller Company merged and formed the Stitzel-Weller Company. It built a new distillery in Shively that opened in 1935. The distillery had 14 warehouses with a total capacity for 220,000 barrels. The plant was sold to Norton Simon Inc. in 1972. It ceased operations in 1992 and is currently owned by Diageo.

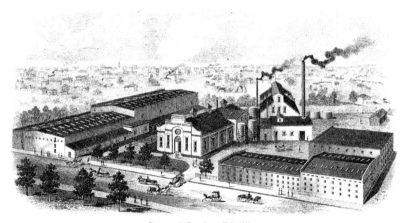

Crystal Spring Distillery

S. C. Herbst Distillery
Courtesy of Capitol City Museum

LAVAL FAMILY
JEFFERSON AND WOODFORD COUNTIES

The Laval family was closely related to the Stitzel family. In 1874, Johann Jacob Laval's daughter, Emma, married Frederick Stitzel, thereby making Emma's brother, Jacob M. Laval, his brother-in-law.

Jacob did business in Louisville in the late 1850s as Schrodt and Laval, rectifiers and distillers. By 1863, he had built the Crystal Spring Distillery, RD #78, at Second Street and Magnolia Avenue in Louisville. The distillery could mash 140 bushels per day and could store 12,700 barrels.

Jacob Laval later built the Garland Distillery, RD #3, at that same location. The distillery could mash 440 bushels a day and had warehouse capacity for 22,000 barrels. Jacob died in 1871, and his oldest son, Charles, took over operation of the distillery until 1880, when it was sold to Jacob's son-in-law, Ferdinand Jaeger.

By 1880, Jacob's son, Jacob M. Laval, had moved to Woodford County and was operating the Johnson Miller Distillery, RD #32, with his younger brother, Ferdinand. The plant was on Griers Creek, near its mouth at the Kentucky River. It later became the Old Barbee Distillery. The distillery could mash about 100 bushels per day and could store 17,500 barrels.

That same year, Jacob M. Laval, Frederick Stitzel, and Christian Stege purchased the Glen Spring Distillery, RD #57. The plant was on Glenns Creek in Woodford County, about four miles northwest of Versailles. It was ultimately sold to the Trust in 1899 and closed.

Around 1890, brothers Jacob M. and Ferdinand Laval, with a Mr. Mayse, purchased the Old Judge Distillery, RD #11, on Benson Creek, just outside of Frankfort. The distillery mashed about 100 bushels per day, and its warehouse capacity was 10,000 barrels. The distillery was sold to S. C. Herbst in about 1900.

H. A. THIERMAN
JEFFERSON COUNTY

H. A. Thierman entered the whiskey business in 1858 as a member of the firm of Thierman and Prande, a wholesale liquor company in Louisville. By 1864, he had purchased the Rugby Distillery, RD #360, also in Louisville, which had been owned by John G. Roach. The plant operated until Prohibition.

In 1884, Thierman and William Ruedeman purchased the Mayflower Distillery, RD #354, from David L. Graves. At that time, the plant was mashing 175 bushels per day. The plant, across Lexington Road from Cherokee Park, was later renamed the Old Kentucky Distillery. Thierman later sold the distillery to Dick Meschendorf.

H. A. Thierman was also a major stockholder in the John T. Barbee Distillery, RD #32, in Woodford County and operated by John T. Barbee. The distillery mashed 100 bushels a day. Thierman died in 1900.

Rugby Distillery

JOHN CALLAGHAN
JEFFERSON COUNTY

John Callaghan got his start in the firm of Callaghan and Trigg, Louisville, in 1870. The wholesale liquor company was in existence from 1870 to 1876. John subsequently established his own firm, which lasted from 1877 to 1889.

During the 1870s, he may have been involved in the Crystal Spring Distillery, RD #78, and in Garland Distillery, RD #3, both of which were in Louisville. By 1882, he and W. S. Harris owned and operated the Kentucky Club Distillery, later known as the Daviess County Distillery, RD #2, in Owensboro. W. S. Harris also was the owner of the White Mills Distillery, RD #414, in Louisville.

In 1880, Callaghan became an owner of the Belle of Marion Distillery, RD #370, in Lebanon. The distillery had a mashing capacity of 300 bushels per day and storage for 25,000 barrels. His partners were Ralph L. Spalding and Charles D. Boldrick. John Callaghan died in 1889.

CUMMINS FAMILY
MARION COUNTY

Richard Cummins came to the United States with his brother Patrick in 1848. He lived initially in New Jersey and then moved to Louisville. His next move was to Bullitt County, where he ran a distillery for a short time, and then he relocated to Illinois with Henry McKenna, where he again ran a distillery.

In 1859, he returned to Kentucky and settled at Raywick in Marion County, where again he operated a distillery. In 1868, he built and operated the Coon Hollow Distillery near New Hope in Nelson County. He later sold that plant and built a second distillery, which he also called the Coon Hollow Distillery, near the train depot of the same name. In 1881, he sold the distillery to the Nelson County Distillery Company, RD #294. The distillery mashed 200 bushels per day and had warehouse storage for 15,000 barrels.

Next, Cummins bought the Ballard and Lancaster Distillery, RD #357, near Loretto in Marion County. It mashed about 100 bushels per day, and its warehouse could store 2,700 barrels. He renamed the plant the R. Cummins Distillery. His son, J. P. Cummins, worked with him at the plant.

Richard was also the third partner in the firm of Mattingly & Moore, RD #272, with Thomas Moore and Benjamin Mattingly. The distillery was just outside Bardstown in Nelson County.

Arthur Cummins, the son of Patrick and nephew of Richard, worked in the distillery at Coon Hollow. Later he moved to the Sam P. Lancaster Distillery, RD #415, and to the Crystal Spring Distillery, RD #78, in Louisville. He subsequently purchased the Willow Springs Distillery, RD #10, in Nelson County. Arthur J., Arthur's son, worked with his

Nelson County Distillery

father at the Willow Spring plant until 1920, when he established the Cummins Distillery, RD #203, in Athertonville, Larue County. He also worked at the Louisville Distillery, RD #408, in Lyndon, just east of Louisville, with both his brother Charles W. and his son, Charles.

THOMAS S. MOORE
NELSON COUNTY

Soon after the Civil War, Thomas S. Moore, John David Willett, and a Mr. Frenke built a distillery just outside of Bardstown. Tom Moore, with Benjamin Mattingly and Richard Cummins, formed the Mattingly & Moore Distillery Company, RD #272, in 1877, and purchased the distillery. The plant could mash 250 bushels per day and could store 7,500 barrels of whiskey.

In 1889, Tom Moore sold his interest in the Mattingly & Moore Distillery and built his own plant, RD #355, next to the distillery. The Tom Moore Distillery had mashing capacity of 100 bushels and storage for 4,500 barrels. This plant operated until Prohibition, after which it was reopened in 1934 by Tom's son, Con. The distillery later became Barton Brands, Ltd., and it is still in operation today as Barton's 1792 Distillery.

In 1899, F. G. Walker retired from his distillery, RD #410, and sold the plant to Tom Moore and R. H. Edelen. This plant could mash 250 bushels per day and could store 14,000 barrels.

Tom Moore Distillery

Mattingly & Moore Whiskey

Mattingly & Moore Distillery

THOMAS H. SHERLEY
JEFFERSON AND NELSON COUNTIES

Thomas H. Sherley entered the whiskey business in 1865 as a distiller's agent and a broker. Within a short period of time, he would control a large number of brands around the state, including two-thirds of all the apple and peach brandy produced in Kentucky.

In the late 1860s, he purchased the Crystal Spring Distillery, RD #78, previously described, from Jacob Laval, who remained as its distiller.

Soon thereafter, Sherley became an owner of the E. L. Miles Distillery, RD #101, at New Hope in Nelson County. Sherley enlarged and improved the plant, whose annual production was 10,000 barrels of sweet mash whiskey. By 1885, the concern had become a stock company with Thomas as its president.

In 1876, Sherley, with E. L. Miles, built a second distillery at the same site, known as the New Hope Distillery, RD #271. At these two distilleries, the well-known brand Belle of Nelson was produced for the Bartley and Johnson Company at the rate of about 6,000 barrels a year.

In 1879, he purchased the Glen Spring Distillery, RD #57, on Glenns Creek in Woodford County. Soon thereafter he sold the distillery to Frederick Stitzel and others.

Thomas H. Sherley was involved in many different endeavors and served as chairman of the Louisville School Board and as a director of the Board of Trade.

George Garvin Brown

BROWN FAMILY
JEFFERSON COUNTY

George Garvin Brown was born in 1846 in Munfordville in Hart County. He moved to Louisville in 1863 and, by 1870, had joined his half-brother, J. T. S. Brown, in the operation of a wholesale liquor business known as J. T. S. Brown and Brother. The firm bought bulk whiskey from several different distillers and blended it into a taste profile to their liking. Although the company was producing a top-rate product; it did not always reach the consumer. They decided to bottle their product to ensure that it would not be tampered with on the way to market. It was an innovation that was years ahead of its time. Simultaneously, they decided to introduce the "Old Forrester" brand, and later changed the spelling to "Old Forester."

George Forman of Paris, Kentucky, was hired in 1872 as a salesman, and later became a bookkeeper. Henry Chambers became a major stockholder in 1873. After J. T. S. Brown left the firm the next year, its name was changed to Brown, Chambers and Company. James Thompson, an Irishman and second cousin of George Brown, and George Forman formed a sales agency to represent Brown, Chambers in 1879. Henry Chambers retired in 1881, selling his interest to Brown. At that point, the name was changed to Brown, Thompson and Company. In 1890, Thompson sold his interest to Brown-Forman and bought the Glenmore Distillery, RD #24, in Owensboro. After George Forman's death in 1901, his interest was purchased by George Brown, and the firm's name remained Brown-Forman.

In 1902, the company purchased a minority interest in the B. F. Mattingly Distillery, RD #14, in St. Mary in Marion County. The distillery had almost no warehousing, so the whiskey was shipped to Louisville and stored at the White Mills Distillery, RD #414, the current site of Brown-Forman. At the time the Mattingly Distillery was purchased, it was mashing 100 bushels per day, and by 1908 that rate had risen to 400 bushels. The B. F. Mattingly Distillery closed at Prohibition.

In 1924, Brown-Forman purchased the White Mills Distillery, which had become a concentration warehouse during Prohibition. Brown-Forman bottled whiskey for medicinal purposes during Prohibition and, in 1933, rebuilt the Lynndale Distillery, RD #470, next to the White Mills plant. After it was rebuilt, the Lynndale plant could mash 6,000 bushels per day and had warehouse storage for 92,000 barrels.

In the early 1920s, the company acquired the brand name and whiskey of the Early Times Distillery, RD #7, formerly in Nelson County. In 1940, Brown-Forman purchased the Old Kentucky Distillery, RD #354, in Shively, just south of Louisville, and renamed it the Early Times Distillery. This plant could mash 1,000 bushels per day and could store 40,000 barrels.

In 1940, Brown-Forman bought the Labrot & Graham Distillery, RD #82, in Woodford County. In the late 1990s, the distillery was rebuilt into a beautiful facility, and it is currently open for tours. It was renamed the Woodford Reserve Distillery about 2010.

In 1956, the company purchased the Jack Daniels Distillery in Lynchburg, Tennessee. Brown-Forman owns the Canadian Mist and Southern brands, and many others.

J. T. S. Brown and Sons purchased the J. M. Waterfill Distillery, RD #2, near McBrayer in Anderson County in 1894. The firm consisted of J. T. S. Brown and his five sons: Graham, Davis, Creel, J. T. S. Jr., and Hewitt. The distillery was renamed the Old Prentice Distillery. The firm built a new plant (in the Spanish mission style) across the road in 1910, and it is currently the site of the Four Roses Distillery, DSP #8. The distillery could mash 500 bushels per day and had warehouse capacity for 40,000 barrels. After Prohibition, the distillery was reopened as the Old Joe Distillery, and one of the owners was Agnes Brown, widow of

White Mills Distillery

Four Roses Distillery

Davis Brown. This plant ultimately became known as the Four Roses Distillery and is in operation today.

In 1935, Creel Brown Jr. rebuilt the original Early Times Distillery, RD #7, outside Bardstown and operated as the J. T. S. Brown Distillery, RD #29. The distillery could mash 200 bushels a day and had storage for 11,000 barrels. The distillery was sold in 1942 to a Cincinnati firm, and it was later purchased by Bob and Alvin Gould of the same city in 1955. Soon thereafter the plant was sold to the Double Springs Distillery, RD #51. The distillery closed in the late 1950s.

The Gould brothers moved the name J. T. S. Brown to the Old Hickory Distillery, RD #6 (formerly the Ripy Brothers Distillery), which they owned in Anderson County. In 1972, they sold the plant to Austin, Nichols and Company, and the name was changed to Wild Turkey. It is still in operation today.

DANT FAMILY
MARION COUNTY

Joseph Washington (J. W.) Dant began distilling in 1836 at Dant Station, named for the family, in Marion County. His first still was a hollow poplar log. J. W. had seven sons—J. Bernard, Thomas Sidney, John P., James R., Wallace W., Frank L., and George W.—and all were involved in the whiskey business. In 1870, he built a modern distillery, RD #169, and, in the 1890s, his sons, Wallace and, later, George, took over the operation of the plant. The distillery could mash about 200 bushels a day and had storage for 3,300 barrels. J. W. ran the distillery for some 61 years.

By 1900, a second distillery was in operation at this location that was owned by the Jesse Moore-Hunt Company of Louisville and operated by the same name, RD #170. This plant could mash about 100 bushels a day, and its warehouse could store 12,500 barrels. The distilleries operated until Prohibition. After Prohibition, the Dant Distillery reopened. Its officers were George W. Dant, president; T. S. Dant, vice-president; and J. E. Dant, secretary and treasurer.

Joseph Bernard (J. B.) Dant built the Cold Spring Distillery, RD #240, at Gethsemane in Nelson County in 1865. This was a small distillery, mashing 70 bushels a day and having storage for 4,500 barrels In the 1880s, the distillery started making the brand Yellowstone, named for the newly formed Yellowstone National Park. Taylor & Williams, a Louisville distribution firm, contracted with the plant to sell its whiskey. In 1892, Taylor retired, and in 1903, Williams died. The firm of Taylor & Williams was reorganized with J. B. Dant as president.

The plant closed at Prohibition, but after its repeal was reopened by Will Dant and Joe B. Head as Rant and Head Distillery, DSP #47. Production was greatly increased, and warehousing was built for 65,000 barrels.

J. B. Dant

Yellowstone Distillery

In 1910, Taylor & Williams, with J. B. Dant as its president, bought the Head and Beam Distillery, RD #405, which was next to the Cold Spring Distillery. This plant could mash 100 bushels and had storage for 8,000 barrels. Both plants were used to make Yellowstone whiskey, which became extremely popular.

In 1855, the Smith and Smith Distillery, RD #11, was purchased by John Proctor Dant. The distillery was located at Chicago (now St. Francis) in Marion County. Its distiller, Thad Dant, could mash about 100 bushels a day. In 1879, the plant was sold to Blair and Ballard, RD #375.

In 1933, J. B. Dant and his six sons—Michael J., J. Walter, Samuel J., Felix R., J. Randolph, and Paul R.—and a nephew, J. P. Kearnes, built the Yellowstone Distillery, RD #240, in Shively, south of Louisville. The plant could mash 1,000 bushels a day and had seven warehouses with capacity of 20,000 barrels each. In 1944, the plant was purchased by Glenmore Distilling Company.

In 1937, John P. Dant Sr., a son of J. W., built a distillery at Meadowlawn in southern Jefferson County. The distiller, and subsequent owner, was John P. Dant Jr. He could mash about 450 bushels per day and had warehouse capacity for 7,500 barrels. The Dants also leased the Grosscurth Distillery, RD #26, near Fisherville in eastern Jefferson County, and ran both distilleries as the Meadowlawn Distillery Company. The plant was later known as the Old Boone Distillery.

Photos above: T. W. Samuels Distillery

SAMUELS FAMILY
NELSON COUNTY

Taylor William (T. W.) Samuels built a distillery near Deatsville in Nelson County in 1844. He and his son, William I., operated the plant until 1898, when both father and son died. At that point, William's son, Leslie B., took over the operation of the distillery. The distillery could mash about 100 bushels a day and could store 9,500 barrels. The plant closed at Prohibition but reopened after its repeal. The company was reorganized with Robert L. Block, president, Leslie B. as vice-president, and Bill Samuels Sr., as manager. In 1936, Leslie died, and Bill Samuels Sr. became vice-president. In 1943, the plant was sold to the Foster Trading Company. The plant closed about 1952.

In 1882, W. I. and T. P. Samuels, sons of T. W., operated a distillery near Sayers Depot, just across the railroad tracks from their father's distillery.

In 1953, Bill Samuels Sr. purchased the Burks Spring Distillery, RD #440, near Loretto in Marion County. The distillery could mash about 200 bushels a day and could store 15,000 barrels. Originally, the plant was named the Old Samuels Distillery, then renamed the Star Hill Distillery and, most recently, Makers Mark Distillery. Bill Jr. joined his father in the business, and when it was sold to Hiram Walker in 1981, Bill Sr. retired. Bill Jr. remained with the company as president until he in turn passed the job on to his son, Rob, in 2011. Bill Jr. was the champion of bourbon for many years, through some of the leanest times during the 1980s and 1990s. The Makers Mark Distillery is very much alive and is well worth a visit.

Taylor W. Samuels
Courtesy of Makers Mark Distillery

Makers Mark Distillery

BEAM FAMILY
NELSON COUNTY

The first Beam distillery was built in 1795 in what was then Washington County but is now Marion County. It was built by Jacob Beam (originally Johannes Jacob Boehm) and in 1818, his son David began operating the distillery. In 1853, David was succeeded by his son, David M. Beam. David M. moved the distillery four miles east of Bardstown. Soon thereafter his son, John Henry (Jack) Beam, became the owner and operator of the plant that was now known as the Early Times Distillery, RD #7. At first, the distillery was mashing 100 bushels per day, but 1891, the plant mashed 600 bushels a day and could store 22,000 barrels. Jack Beam died in 1915, as did his son Edward D. Beam a few months later. The distillery closed at Prohibition, and the Early Times brand name was sold to Brown-Forman in Louisville.

In 1860, David M. Beam built a new plant about two miles northwest of Bardstown, known as the Clear Spring Distillery, RD #230. By 1882 the distillery was being run by his son, James Beauregard (Jim) Beam, and David's son-in-law, Albert J. Hart, and it was known as the Beam and Hart Distillery. Its most famous brand was Old Tub, and the plant was sometimes known by that name. At that time the distillery was mashing 300 bushels a day and had warehouse capacity for 11,000 barrels. The plant closed at Prohibition but was reopened upon its repeal as the Bardstown Distillery, RD #4.

In 1883, Minor Case (M. C.) Beam purchased the Francis M. Head Distillery, RD #47, at Gethsemane in Nelson County. M. C. was the grandson of David M. Beam and the son of Joseph B. Beam, and he had been the distiller at the Early Times Distillery. The plant mashed 100 bushels a day and could store 5,500 barrels. In 1910, the plant was sold to Taylor & Williams to make the Yellowstone brand.

During Prohibition, the James B. Beam Company, with Jim Beam as president, purchased the Murphy, Barber Distillery, RD #401, at Clermont in Bullitt County. It was reopened as the Jim Beam Distillery, RD #230. The plant could mash 665 bushels per day and had warehousing for 160,000 barrels. Jim died in 1947 at age 83, and T. Jeremiah Beam became president. F. Booker Noe Jr., his nephew and Jim's grandson, was plant manager. The plant is still in operation and is one of Kentucky's largest.

In 1953, the James B. Beam Company purchased the Churchill Downs Distillery, RD #13, in Boston, Nelson County, and Booker Noe was its distiller. The plant has the capacity to mash about 850 bushels a day and storage for 48,000 barrels. It is still in production today.

In 1970, the company purchased the Limestone Springs Distillery, RD #18, for additional warehousing. In 1971, it purchased the Bardstown Distillery, RD #4, for storage but, in the 1990s, sold it to Heaven Hill. In 1974, the company bought the Waterfill-Frazier Distillery, DSP #28, near Bardstown for storage. In 1985, Beam acquired the Old Crow Distillery, RD #06, for warehousing only and, at about the same time, bought the Old Grand-Dad Distillery, DSP #14, near Frankfort for storage and for its bottling facilities. The company currently has storage facilities for over two million barrels.

Only the distilleries in which the Beam family had an ownership interest have been mentioned. While the family has produced countless distillers at many of Kentucky's finest distilleries, no attempt has been made to name them in this work.

Churchill Downs Distillery

Jim Beam Distillery

Early Times Distillery

Thomas Beebe Ripy

Ripy Brothers Distillery
Courtesy of University of Kentucky

RIPY FAMILY
ANDERSON COUNTY

In the late 1830s, two brothers, John and James Ripy, left their home in Tyrone County, Ireland, and settled in Anderson County. James had two sons who were prominent in the whiskey business, James P. Ripy and Thomas Beebe (T. B.) Ripy. T. B. Ripy had nine children. Five of them—T. B. Jr., Ezra, Ernest, Robert, and Forrest—were involved in distilling.

In 1868, Walker, Martin and Company, whose principals were Monroe Walker, Sam P. Martin, and James Ripy, purchased a distillery, RD #112, on Bailey's Run, at its mouth on the Kentucky River, about four miles southeast of Lawrenceburg. The next year, the distillery was sold to T. B. Ripy and W. H. McBrayer. By 1870, T. B. had bought McBrayer's interest and become the sole owner of the distillery, which was known as both the T. B. Ripy Distillery and the Cliff Springs Distillery. By 1890, its mashing capacity was 1,500 bushels per day, and its warehouse could store 67,000 barrels.

In 1881, J. W. Waterfill, the Dowling Brothers, and T. B. Ripy built a second distillery, RD #418, next to RD #112. By 1885, T. B. had purchased the interest of both of his partners and become the sole owner of the plant. This plant could mash 1,259 bushels a day and had storage for 38,000 barrels. By the 1890s, these two plants had become two of the largest whiskey distilleries in the world. The plant was known as both the Anderson County Sour Mash Distillery and the Clover Bottom Distillery. Both distilleries were sold to the Whiskey Trust in 1899.

James P. Ripy entered the Confederate Army and served under General John Hunt Morgan. After the war, he returned to Lawrenceburg, and in 1888 he purchased a distillery on the cliffs overlooking the Kentucky River and renamed it the Old Hickory Distillery, RD #6. The plant could mash 165 bushels a day and had storage for 9,500 barrels. In 1906, the distillery was reorganized and renamed the Ripy Brothers Distillery. Ezra was president; James P., vice-president; and Forrest, secretary and treasurer. The distillery reopened after Prohibition in 1937 as Ripy Brothers, but was later purchased by Alvin and Bob Gould and renamed the J. T. S. Brown Distillery. In 1972, the plant was sold to Austin, Nichols and Company, and it is now known as the Wild Turkey Distillery.

James P. Ripy also owned the James P. Ripy Distillery, RD #5, on the Kentucky River near Tyrone. The plant was built about 1882 and operated until about 1901, when it was sold to the Trust. The distillery mashed 500 bushels a day and could store 13,000 barrels.

T. B. Ripy purchased the Old Joe Distillery, RD #45, in 1885 and sold it a short time later to Wiley Searcy. In 1911, the Ripy Brothers once again purchased the plant, selling it soon thereafter. The distillery was on Gilbert's Creek, near its mouth at the Kentucky River.

T. B. Ripy also purchased the Edward Murphy Distillery, RD #400, in the early 1880s, and later sold it to Murphy and Dowling. This distillery was on a bluff overlooking the Kentucky River, north of Lawrenceburg.

Robert and Ezra Ripy, sons of T. B., rebuilt the Hoffman Distillery, RD #12, after Prohibition. The plant was on Hammond Creek in Anderson County, Lawrenceburg. This distillery was purchased by the Medleys in the 1970s.

James P. Ripy bought the J. W. Stevens Distillery, RD #416, in 1891, and later sold it to J. S. Searcy. The distillery was near Shiloh in Anderson County.

ROBERT AND ALVIN A. GOULD
CINCINNATI, OHIO

The Gould brothers are among the few exceptions to the Bourbon Barons who operated distilleries before Prohibition. They are also the only Barons who did not live in Kentucky. Although they were from Ohio, Robert and Alvin were involved in at least six different distilleries in Kentucky during a relative brief period.

During the late 1940s, the brothers owned the Dowling Brothers Distillery, RD #148, near Burgin in Mercer County. The distillery could mash 300 bushels per day and could store 20,000 barrels. They sold the plant to Schenley Distilleries, Inc. for $10 million. The brothers operated it as the J. T. S. Brown Distillery Company.

Soon after selling the Dowling Brothers Distillery, they sold the Cave Spring Distillery, which was later known as the Pebbleford Distillery, DSP #34. This plant was near Wilder in Campbell County. It could mash 850 bushels a day and had warehousing for 20,400 barrels.

The brothers purchased the Greenbrier Distillery, RD #239, in the early 1950s, and it operated as the Double Springs Distillery. The plant was in Nelson County, near Woodlawn. It could mash 1,200 bushels a day and could store 58,000 barrels.

In 1955, Creel Brown sold the J. T. S. Brown Distillery, RD #9, to the brothers. The plant was four miles east of Bardstown, on the site of the Early Times Distillery, RD #7. In 1956, the Goulds moved the name to Anderson County, where they had bought the Old Hickory Distillery, RD #6, from the Ripy brothers. This plant later became the Wild Turkey Distillery, RD #27, and it is still in operation today.

In the 1950s, the Goulds purchased the Bonds Mill Distillery, RD #35, which was in Anderson County and directly across the road from the Four Roses Distillery, DSP #8. The distillery mashed 300 bushels a day.

DOWLING BROTHERS
MERCER AND ANDERSON COUNTIES

The Dowling brothers, Edward, John, and Michael, purchased the D. L. Moore Distillery, RD #23 and #148, in 1889. The plant was five miles east of Harrodsburg in Mercer County. At that time the plant could mash 250 bushels a day and had warehouse capacity for 15,000 barrels. The distillery was reopened after Prohibition in 1934, by Herbert P. Dowling, Edward's son.

In 1883, Edward Murphy and Michael Dowling purchased a distillery in Anderson County that became known as the Murphy and Dowling Distillery, RD #400. At that time it could mash 200 bushels a day and had warehouse storage for 10,000 barrels. The plant was nine miles northeast of Lawrenceburg, on the Kentucky River. Dowling sold his interest to Murphy in 1888.

In 1903, John Dowling built a new distillery on the site of the old J. M. Walker Distillery, RD #166, which was known as the John Dowling Distillery, RD #59. It was one mile northeast of Lawrenceburg. It could mash 100 bushels a day and could store 15,000 barrels. John died shortly after the distillery was built, and his widow, Mary M. Dowling, took over its operation.

In the mid 1880s, John Dowling was a member of the firm of Waterfill, Dowling and Company, which had purchased the Waterfill-Frazier Distillery, RD #41. The plant was on Bailey's Run near Tyrone, on the Kentucky River. The distillery could mash 100 bushels a day and had warehouse capacity for 9,000 barrels. Upon John's death, the distillery was owned by his widow, Mary, and run by his son, William.

After Prohibition, in 1933, John Dowling built a new distillery, also known as the Waterfill-Frazier Distillery, RD #26. The plant was near

D. L. Moore Distillery
Courtesy of Oscar Getz Museum

Fisherville, in Jefferson County, on Echo Creek. The distillery could mash 400 bushels a day and had storage for 35,000 barrels of whiskey. The plant was later sold to Charles A. Grosscurth, who leased it to John P. Dant.

Belmont Distillery

Astor Distillery

JESSE AND GEORGE H. MOORE
JEFFERSON COUNTY

Jesse Moore and his brother George J. Moore moved to Louisville from Worcester, Massachusetts, in the 1830s. Late in the decade, George J. invested in a distillery in Mt. Vernon, Indiana, which they renamed the Phoenix. Jesse was put in charge of its operation, and by 1843, Jesse had purchased a 40 percent ownership in the plant. In the late 1840s, the brothers sold the distillery and returned to Louisville.

They established a liquor brokerage firm in 1860, and in 1866, Jesse and his nephew, George J.'s son George H. Moore, founded Jesse Moore and Company. In 1875, they built the Belmont Distillery, RD #1, and soon thereafter, the Astor Distillery, RD #2, both at 17th and Breckinridge Street in Louisville. The Belmont Distillery produced a sour mash product and could mash 760 bushels per day. The Astor made a sweet mash whiskey and could mash 725 bushels a day. The plants could store a total of 42,000 barrels.

The company sold a great deal of whiskey on the West Coast and founded the firm of Jesse Moore-Hunt and Company to operate there. That firm built a distillery next to the J. W. Dant Distillery in Marion County in the late 1890s. It was known as the Jesse Moore-Hunt Distillery, RD #169. This plant could mash 100 bushels a day and had warehouse capacity for 12,500 barrels. Jesse retired in 1892 and George H., in 1898.

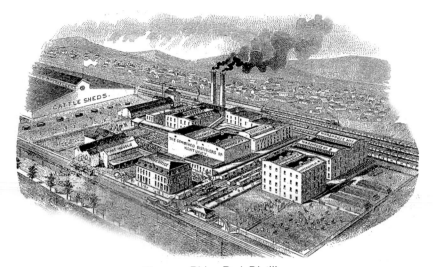

Pleasure Ridge Park Distillery
Courtesy of Filson Historical Society

I. W. Harper

BERNHEIM BROTHERS AND NATHAN URI
JEFFERSON COUNTY

Isaac and Bernard Bernheim and Nathan Uri, Isaac's brother-in-law, all of Paducah, formed a liquor brokerage firm in 1872. Nathan's father had been an owner of a distillery near New Hope in Nelson County.

By 1888, they had purchased the Pleasure Ridge Park Distillery, RD #413, in Jefferson County and in the community of the same name. The plant could mash about 450 bushels a day and could store 30,000 barrels.

In the 1890s, Uri sold his interest in the company and purchased the Gwyn Springs Distillery, RD #31, near Bardstown in Nelson County. The distillery could mash 65 bushels per day and store 4,500 barrels.

Around the turn of the century, the Bernheim brothers sold the Pleasure Ridge Park Distillery and built a large plant in Shively, in Jefferson County. The Bernheim Distillery, RD #9, could mash 600 bushels a day, and its warehouse capacity was about 60,000 barrels. The distillery's premium brand was I. W. Harper.

In 1906, the Bernheims purchased the Warwick Distillery, RD #23, near Silver Creek in Madison. The distillery could mash 600 bushels a day and had storage for 9,200 barrels.

The brothers purchased 14,000 acres of land in Bullitt County, where they created a preserve known today as Bernheim Forest, and made it a gift to the Commonwealth of Kentucky. The brothers made a gift of the Thomas Jefferson statue that stands in front of the Jefferson County Courthouse (now Louisville Metro Hall). Two other gifts, bronze statues of Henry Clay and Ephraim McDowell, are in Statuary Hall in Washington, DC. The brothers never forgot their humble backgrounds and gave many monetary gifts to organizations throughout Kentucky.

AUTHOR'S NOTE

My purpose in writing this book has been to show the relationship of those titans of the industry who were involved in multiple distilling operations. Many of the individuals or families mentioned were forgotten long ago because none of their surviving family members have carried on the distilling tradition and thus kept the family names in the public eye. I sincerely hope you have enjoyed this brief look back into Kentucky's glorious distilling past.

—Chester Zoeller

ABOUT THE AUTHOR

Chester "Chet" Zoeller was born in Louisville, Kentucky, in 1941. He was raised in the shadow of Churchill Downs and lived within a few short blocks of many of the largest distilleries of the day; the Yellowstone, Seagram's, Hill and Hill, and Stitzel-Weller distilleries were all within smelling distance.

Mr. Zoeller attended the University of Kentucky before earning his undergraduate degree from Western Kentucky University and his law degree from the University of Louisville. He practiced law for a number of years in Louisville before purchasing and operating a telecommunications firm in Savannah, Georgia. After he returned to Louisville, in 1997 he established the McLain and Kyne Distillery Company with his son, Trey. They produced several brands of bourbon—Jefferson's, Jefferson's Reserve, and Jefferson's Rye.

Interested in the history of the whiskey business in Kentucky, Mr. Zoeller began researching the subject, which led to his writing *Bourbon in Kentucky: A History of Distilleries in Kentucky*, originally published in 2009. He has since updated and revised the book twice. His second book, *Kentucky Bourbon Barons*, introduces readers to the giants in the industry during the golden years of distilling.

Mr. Zoeller travels the country giving talks on the history of bourbon and Kentucky's distilleries.